C0-APJ-267

How To Keep More of What You Make!

135 EASY WAYS TO SAVE MONEY AND INCREASE YOUR PURCHASING POWER!

By Doris Fitzgerald
With Brett Birdsong

Words of Wisdom Press
Everett, Washington

www.wordsofwisdompress.com
www.howtokeepmoreofwhatyoumake.com
www.dorisfitz.com

© 2003 by Doris Fitzgerald

All rights reserved. No portion of this work may be reproduced, stored in a retrieval system or transmitted in any form or by any means including electronic, mechanical, photo reproduction, audio recording or any other device as yet unknown with out the express written consent of the copyright holder.

Published by
Words of Wisdom Press

Design, Layout and Cartoons by
Brett Birdsong, www.birdsongnw.com

International Standard Book Number (ISBN)
0-9743590-0-9

Printed in the United States of America

1st Edition

For Drew,
who treats me like a queen.

Contents

For I know the plans
I have for you,
declares the Lord.
Plans to prosper you
and not to harm you,
plans to give you a
hope and a future.
Jeremiah 29:11 NIV

A Love Letter from The Heart of God

My dear child:

How can you doubt that I love you when I've sent my word? I told you that I loved you, and you doubt that it's true. How can you say that, when I've sent my Word to you? My love song is in each book reaching out to you, my sonnet is on each page saying "I love you." Last but not least, I sent my Son to set you free. He was ridiculed and maimed for you, but I knew his blood would wash over you and make you mine, so it was worth it.

I have given you forever and it was signed with my blood. I've given you authority to have all, by using my word. I've given you power and help by my spirit always walking and talking to you, if you will listen, you will never die.I have given you forever and it was signed with my blood. I have done everything to protect you that I can.

You are mine, my loved one whose very righteousness comes from me, whose very existence comes from me, I will and have fought for thee. I have sent my servants, the angels, to protect you.

My spirit and word guide you with love. In my love are all things accomplished. Praise me! For in praise to me will my love flow in you, and all things will be accomplished as my word says. Remember I love you, and care for you. I have given you forever and signed it with my blood.

Father

The preceding love letter was a message God had for me when I was going through a time of trouble and doubt. I've included it here as testimony to the protection, provision and purpose God has had on my life since that time. I've made just about every financial mistake you can make, but he helped me to recover, and now I want to share what I've learned with you. I hope you will get a sense of his purpose for your life.

FORWARD

How would you like to give yourself a ten percent raise? Right now, today. Would you do it if you could? Sure you would! Most likely, you can't just give yourself a raise in *gross* income, (unless, of course, you're a member of Congress) but you can increase your *effective* income!

What is your effective income? Of course, your gross income is the total amount of your paycheck before taxes, while your net income is what you have left over after the government finishes with you. However, your effective income is the *value* squeezed out of your net income. This book shows you how to make your net income more effective and more valuable by presenting practical, money saving tips on everything from taxes to groceries.

Warning: Financial Principles work both ways.

The principles outlined in this book will work either for you or against you. If you ignore them, the detrimental effects will continue to eat away at your effective income as if you had holes in your pockets. Nothing in your finances will get better, and you will always feel out of control.

However, if you apply these principles, life will open to you like the red rose of the valley. Bluebirds will sing from the trees. The sun will shine upon you. Honor, riches and glory will rain down on your head. Your vision for the future will come true. Ok, I'm spreading it on a little thick. The point is, your finances will definitely improve! You will have cash available to begin making your dreams come true. Whether you are trying to squeeze out the payment for a new car, find cash for a vacation, or begin building your retirement account, this book can help you sew up the "holes in your pockets" and use your income more effectively.

How to use this book:

Read the book with a highlighter, a note pad and a pen near by. When you run across a concept or tip that relates to your situation, highlight it, and write it down. Soon you will have a list of tips pertaining to you. Choose one or two, and apply those principles to your daily life.

Once your new behavior becomes second nature, move on to the next tip and begin the process over. In a couple of months, you will find that you have changed your spending habits, that you make better financial decisions and that your money works more effectively than ever before.

God bless you,
Doris Fitzgerald.

P.S.

I'm very interested in knowing what you think of the material in this book. Please visit my website at ***www.howtokeepmoreofwhatyoumake.com***, and leave a review of the book, or let me know how it has helped you save money and increase your purchasing power. Or maybe you have some money saving tips of your own to share. You might even see your tip in the next edition of this book!

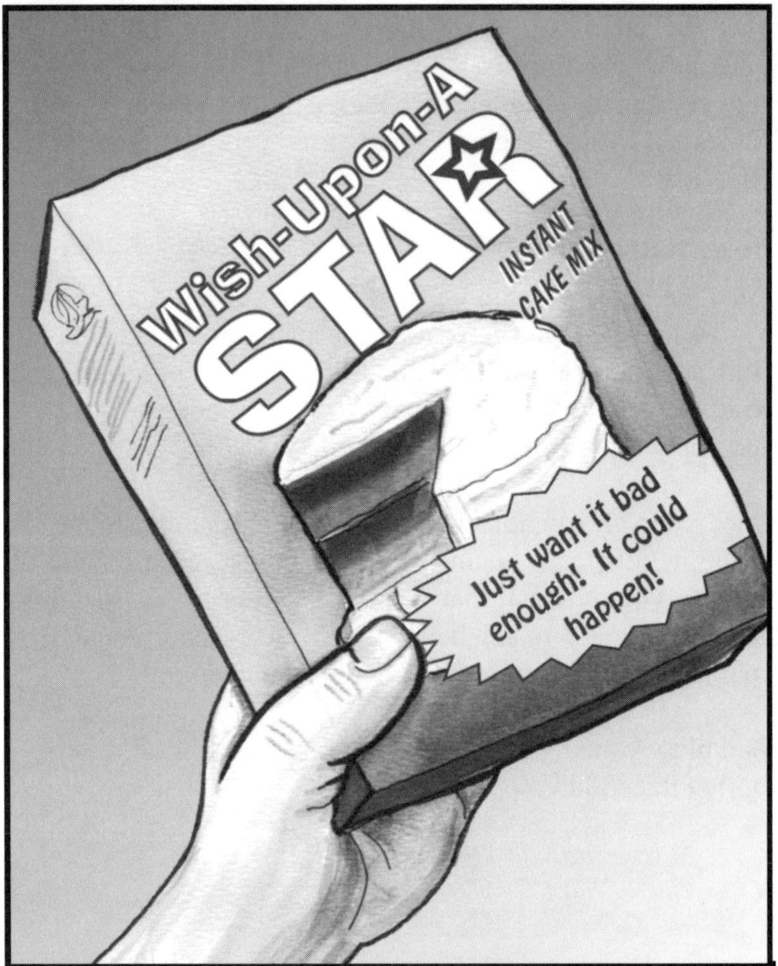

At last, Bob had found the perfect instant cake mix, requiring no actual effort.

INTRODUCTION

Almost everyone nurtures a dream of some kind: a wish-upon-a-star that makes every day life easier to handle, and gives you something to hope for. For instance, you may want to buy your first home, remodel the one you have or build a new home. Yet, sometimes a dream can be so big it seems impossible. You begin to ask, "Can it ever come true? Or, how do I get from here, to there?"

To illustrate the answer to these questions, let's set aside the enormity of building your dream home, and think about achieving a more modest goal: Let's bake a cake!

A cake is a simple thing to make, isn't it? Just grab a cake mix, add some water, a couple of eggs, bake it, frost it and eat it, right? Perhaps not quite. We've glossed over a bunch of steps and left others out completely. It sounds as if, even for baking a cake, we need a plan. Let's look at the steps involved in baking a cake.

Step One: Imagine your cake

The first thing to do is to make some basic decisions about the pending cake. What size will it be? What shape, flavor and color will it have? What flavor of frosting? How will you decorate it? Think of every possible attribute of your cake. Be specific. Make it clear in your mind. In so doing, your daydream becomes your vision of the future cake.

Step Two: Plan your cake

Now you have a clear vision of the cake. Good. Do you have a cake yet? No. You don't even have a recipe for the cake yet. So, now you must break down your vision into specific measurable steps. These steps, combined with deadlines, become your goals for achieving cakeness. Your vision has become a set of measurable goals with a timeline for completion.

Step Three: Count the cost of the cake

Now that you know all the steps in making the cake, and you know all the specifications for the cake, you must determine the cost of the cake. If the cost triggers your gag reflex, relax; just adjust some of your expectations. Use a cake mix instead of imported hand-ground Italian flour, for example.

Step Four: Collect the ingredients

Now that you have a plan and a budget, it's time to put your plan into action. The first step is to gather all of the ingredients listed on your recipe. This may take some time. Especially if you have to wait for that imported flour. For now, let's assume the flour is on hand, and all is in readiness. Your ingredients, pans, whisks and beaters are assembled on your counter top. Do you have a cake yet? No. All you have is cake potentiality, but, you *are* ready to act!

Step Five: Beat the batter

Time to break some eggs. Add the vanilla (imported from Brazil) and the brown sugar. It's starting to smell good enough to eat! In fact, you could just eat the batter, but if you do, you won't achieve your goal: a light, fluffy, moist cake with your favorite frosting. If you stop here, you settle for second best, so pour the batter into the pan and get ready to turn up the heat!

Step Six: Into the oven

Now it's time to shove your carefully prepared batter into the oven, preheated to 350 degrees. Oh, that's hot! Isn't there an easier way to achieve cakeness? Nope. The heat causes the batter to form long molecules from the flour, milk and eggs. Meanwhile, the yeast converts the sugar into carbon dioxide and causes the batter to rise. Leave it in the heat and let it become the cake that it wants to be.

Step Seven: Cool it!

This is the hardest part of making a cake. The cooling off period. You must let the cake cool down. Those long cake molecules are still forming up, and need to take some time to cool off before you spread frosting on them. In addition, the heat will melt your frosting causing it to slide off the sides like the brand X syrup in an Aunt Jemima commercial.

Step Eight: Frost and decorate your cake

At last, the waiting is over. The cake is cool enough to frost and decorate. Through planning and careful attention to detail, you have created a cake where once there had been only a group of unrelated cake parts. The dream that became a vision that was broken down into steps and goals that were turned into actions has become a reality. Congratulations. If you can make a cake, you can turn any of your dreams into realities.

What's it mean master?

Let me explain my little parable. The cake represents your dream. Each of the steps in making the cake correlates to a step in making your dream come true.

How To Keep More of What you Make!

Dreaming in color

Like the cake, dreams will remain nothing but wishes and desires until you start down the road that led to our finished cake. In step one, we made some decisions about the qualities our cake would have. Therefore, the first step of dream fulfillment is to imagine exactly what you want. State it in concrete terms. For example: I want a four bedroom house in a quiet neighborhood. It should be at least 2200 square feet, have a two car garage, gas heat, a large yard and a fireplace in the family room. You get the picture.

Planning the work

Step two is breaking down the vision into measurable pieces that have deadlines attached. These are called goals. A goal should be something achievable. If you find it is not achievable, break it down into smaller goals.

Counting the cost

The next step is to count the cost, and decide what you have to do to reach your goal. Identify the missing parts. Do you need to save more money? (This book will help with that.) Do you need a better job? Should you scale back your dream, or break it into phases? This step is critical. If you don't count your costs, you could wind up like the man who started to build a mansion, and had to stop when he ran out of funds. He became the joke of the neighborhood.

Lining up resources

Working from your master plan, now you must gather the ingredients, or the resources you need to achieve the plan. What outside supplies or services do you need to complete each step of the plan? When do you need them to be on hand? Are there any show-stoppers that will delay your project if they fail to arrive on time? What contingency plans can you make to minimize the effects of missing materials or services? Failure to answer these questions could derail your plans.

Working the plan

Once your planning, funding and resources are in place, drive forward with all your strength. This is the batter of the cake. Work your plan and don't get off course. Begin putting all the parts together. Its exciting to see things come together, but don't waste time admiring the half finished project. Get on with it!

Taking the heat

Step six, the oven, represents all those people who will try to stop your plan. It has always amazed me the number of people who like to tear down what others are building. You will face opposition from almost every quarter.

Friends and family can be especially helpful in pointing out exactly why your plans can never succeed. Don't worry about it. By attacking your plan, they will actually help you succeed. The weaknesses they point out can be eliminated, leaving your plan stronger. Don't short cut this process. On the other hand, don't stay in the oven longer than necessary, or you'll get burned.

Waiting room

The cooling off period represents the processes that are out of your control, like building permits or loan processing time. You just have to wait. There may be little you can do about it, so just be patient, and let the process work.

Celebrating victory!

And the frosting represents the joy of seeing a job through to completion. It's moving-in day. It's the unpacking process. It's arranging the furniture. It's hanging the pictures, and welcoming your first dinner guests. Congratulations. One of your biggest dreams has just come true!

Dreams are important to us. They are the starting point of every thing we do. Left to themselves, however, dreams can come to nothing.

Only by defining a dream does it become a vision for the future. Only by breaking down the vision into manageable steps can you set goals. Only by counting the cost of the goals, can you commit to action. Only by acting to achieve those goals can you realize your dreams.

This book falls into the "counting the cost" part of the process. It's about focusing the power of your money on the completion of your goals. It's about making choices that release the most money to spend on your goals, helping you "bake your cake."

Dreams become
visions.
Visions become
goals.
Goals become
actions.
Actions become
Reality.

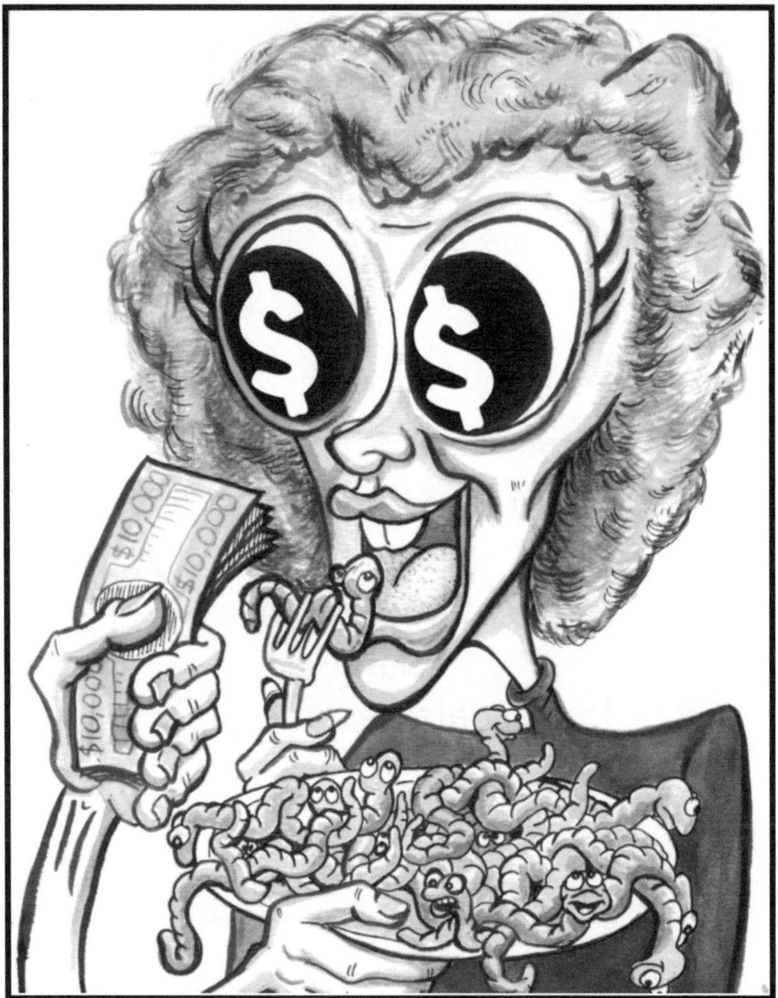

Silvia always had trouble keeping her perspective where money was concerned.

A BALANCED ATTITUDE TOWARDS MONEY

Many people have a distorted attitude towards money. Some love to point out that money can't buy happiness. Others place all their hopes in making as much money as possible, in any way possible. Still others declare money is evil, and those who have money are themselves evil.

So, what's the right perspective on money?

Money is very important.

Money is so important, the major religions of the world spend a great deal of time on the subject. For instance the Bible talks a lot about earning money, saving it, giving it away, spending it and treating it appropriately. It is clear we should take this subject seriously.

Money is not evil

The idea that money is evil is a misreading of the Biblical verse that reads, *"For the **love** of money is a root of all kinds of evil."*[1] The unbalanced longing after the accumulation of wealth for its own sake **is** evil, because it causes us to do evil things, like lying, cheating, stealing, or becoming contestants on reality TV shows.

Money = You

Your money represents your life's energy, time and labor. What ever your income source, energy went into creating the money you live on. If you work for a living, you've traded thousands of hours of your labor to earn the money you have.

Even if you derive all your income from a portfolio of investments, you have bet your own energy on the energy and industry of thousands of other people. For that, your reward is a small amount from each.

If money represents the very life in your body, it only makes sense that you would want to keep as much of it as possible to use as you see fit.

Money is just a tool

Money may not be able to buy happiness, or peace, or joy, but it can certainly help free up your time to concentrate on those things. Money is simply a tool to help you convert your expertise, energy and time into necessities, toys and dreams. Use the tool wisely, and you will always have enough. Use it foolishly, and you will never be able to make enough.

SELFISH HORDING VS. RESPONSIBLE HANDLING

This book is not about piling up huge amounts of cash just so you can let it sit in your bank account, or lie stuffed between the mattresses. There's not much fun in just looking at your money. (Well, actually, it is kind of fun at first, but then, it gets sort of boring.) This book is about pinching pennies in the morning so that your dollars will serenade you at night. It's about setting goals, planning, and learning practical ways to save for that future.

Some of what I have to say here may seem a little strange to you. Some of it may seem nit picky or a little extreme. That's ok. If your aim is to save money to buy a new home, or a car, or to send a child to college, this book has down-to-earth, practical suggestions for you.

I don't want you to turn your life into a dreary regimen of penny-pinching, scrimping and saving with no payoff. I'm saying that the quickest way to a payoff is to know how to do the penny-pinching, scrimping and saving when you need to.

It's about personal responsibility.

Personal responsibility seems to be an outmoded concept these days. In an era when more and more people are looking to the government to take care of their problems, the idea that adults should care for their own needs can sound foreign.

How To Keep More of What you Make!

Unfortunately, we have a large section of the population who are reaching their forties and fifties who never had to grow up. As a baby boomer, I know our parents tried to shield us from the hardships they went through. They lived through the depression and World War II, and so they wanted us to have a better life.

The only problem is that, in never letting us face the tough problems on our own, we grew to depend on mommy and daddy to bail us out of those problems. Moreover, whenever they couldn't do it, we turned to the government to do so. This has led to an entire generation of American adults who still act as though they are teenagers.

If you are to have true financial independence, if you really plan to retire in comfort, then you must come to the realization that you are the one responsible for making it happen.

Social Security may or may not be around when you retire. Even if it is around the monthly income will be just enough to ensure you stay below the poverty line. We must face the fact that government programs are failing to meet the needs of the current recipients, and will not be able to meet the needs of future applicants.

Right now is the time to do something about your future. Putting off the establishment of a savings plan only diminishes your pay off.

A friend of mine turned 40 a year and a half ago. It was a real eye opener for him. He suddenly realized that in only twenty-five years, he would be retiring, and that he didn't have a plan for it. He decided he'd better do something about it. However, he keeps putting off action because he believes he doesn't have any additional money to start a savings program. Sadly, he still hadn't started saving by his 41st birthday, and to my knowledge, has yet to start. Maybe he thinks he will hit the lotto, or suddenly come into wealth that will take care of him and his family.

The truth is, with out a plan for retirement, you will have no retirement. This book is about showing you where the savings can come from by freeing up more of your effective income. You see, if my friend could squeeze out just an extra dollar a day to put into mutual funds for his retirement, he could save $86,280.73 by the time he retires. The problem is, he's not putting anything away right now, because he doesn't know where it would come from. (My example is based upon putting $31 per month into a mutual fund that averaged 15% return over 24 years.)

You, however, are obviously a very smart person! (You bought this book didn't you?) You can see the value of saving for your future. But, just for fun, let's put it in black and white for you. If I could show you how to squeeze out, not just one dollar, but if I could show you how to squeeze out ten dollars a day, and you put it into a mutual fund that averaged 15% return every year for the next 25 years, you could have $1,005,494.18 saved up for your retirement. Yes, $310 per month, for 25 years earning 15% interest is over ONE MILLION dollars! I'd like you to notice, that these figures are not unattainable. Most likely, $310 is much less than ten percent of your monthly income. At a minimum you should be putting away ten percent for yourself. Twenty-five years allows even 40 year olds to take advantage of the magic of compound interest, and 15% is the average annual return for mutual funds over the last fifty years! These are rock solid numbers. The only real variable is your resolve to discipline your self to save just $10 per day and put it into your retirement account.

It's also about personal integrity.

This book offers you a wide range of tips on keeping as much of what you earn as possible, but don't let yourself become unbalanced and lose your personal integrity. There are lots of ways to keep more of your money that are unethical. For instance, the difference between avoiding taxes and evading taxes is critical to understand. One is legal and saves you money, the other is illegal and will land you in jail. In addition to big things like tax evasion, there are the little things like everyday honesty.

Later on I talk about the importance of using coupons for grocery shopping. I love coupons. I play a game of seeing how many coupons I can use in a shopping trip. Unfortunately, I found myself getting a little too aggressive with my coupons, and now I check myself to make sure I'm not being dishonest with them.

I'll make a little confession here. I used to take the soap from the hotel rooms I stayed in. Not, just the ones I used while at the hotel, I would take all of the soaps, shampoos and conditioners on the countertop. You may not think there is anything wrong with that. But one day I was struck by the conviction that I shouldn't be taking more than what I used at the hotel. It was a heart issue for me. Was I so engrossed in saving money, that I had to squeeze out the last bar of soap from a hotel visit? Don't loose your personal integrity in your efforts to save money, or reach your goals. After all, even if you gain the whole world, but lose yourself, what do you have left?

PLANNING YOUR SUCCESS

Underpinning every successful venture is a plan. The success of a project is often determined by the quality and depth of the planning and the execution of the plan.

God is a planner.

God works through processes. He sets things in motion and allows the processes to continue until they produce the end result. He's also a God of miracles, he can skip the process if he chooses to. Yet even in the miraculous, God seems to follow an order. He often tells us before hand what will happen through prophesy, and then he sets in motion the events that will keep his word.

However, most often he simply allows his own principles and processes to progress to completion.

Throughout the world, we see the results of natural processes at work. For example, you must plant a seed before it can grow. At first, it seems that planting ten percent of your seeds means you are now short ten percent of your seeds. In reality, it means that you will soon harvest sixty to one hundred times the amount that you planted, once the growing season is over.

God expects us to be planners.

We have numerous examples in the Bible that demonstrate the importance of planning in our daily lives. When Joseph interpreted the dreams of Pharaoh to mean that seven years of extreme famine would follow seven years of plenty, he advised Pharaoh to start a savings plan in the good years to carry the nation though the bad years.

In the 1930's Walt Disney produced a cartoon called *The Ant and the Grasshopper*. The ants gather their food in the summer and harvest time, allowing them to party all winter. The grasshopper however, gathers nothing, and in time of need finds himself out in the cold. This retelling of Aesop's fable has application for us today. As the Bible puts it: *"Go to the ant, you sluggard; consider its ways and be wise!"* [2]

Seasons of plenty are to be used to prepare for seasons of want. If you have a good job right now, you should be saving for the time when a layoff leaves you wondering what to do next. You need a contingency plan for the times when things don't go as planned. What do you do if you get laid off? This is a huge question right now as our country is experiencing massive layoffs in almost every sector of the economy. However, most people in the country do not plan for the times they are out of work.

If you are in that situation right now, and are thinking, great, I'm laid off, and I didn't make any plans for it, what do I do? The first thing I'd say to you is make a plan for getting the job you want. The second thing I'd say is, work your plan until you've got your new job!

Simple solution, Hard implementation.

The solution to financial problems is simple, just choose to do what is right. Simple to say, but hard to do. Making the right choices all the time isn't easy. So, just start out making more right choices than you make right now. Outlined in this book are over 135 specific tips that will save you money. Some will save you thousands over a year, some hundreds, some only tens. However, as you begin to make these principles your own, you will see a huge difference in what you are able to keep from your net income.

For example, I have a friend who was addicted to his debit card. Nearly every day he would buy something with it: Breakfast, lunch, dinners (ok, maybe it was a food addiction) but my point is, when he surrendered his cash card to his spouse, and went on an allowance, he found he was saving $80 to $120 per month. That's like receiving a $1000 annual raise, simply by putting into practice one of the principles in this book.

Just imagine the possibilities as you incorporate more and more of these principles in your daily life.

Just before dropping this subject, let me just say: get started. Start small if you have to. You don't have to do everything at once. Just start with one or two things, and work them until they are second nature. Then add more.

The Big Secret to Earning and Keeping More Money: GIVE IT AWAY!

Give it away. Give it to your church, give it to the Boy Scouts of America, give it to the guy standing on the street corner with a sign around his neck. Haven't you ever heard that it is better to give than to receive?

The Bible tells us that it is more blessed to give than to receive. *"Give and it will be given to you. A good measure, pressed down, shaken together and running over, will be poured into your lap. For with the measure you use, it will be measured out to you!"*[3]

There is a fundamental principle of the universe that God has set in motion and revealed to us through the Bible: If you give, He will pay you back. If a man borrows ten bucks from you, don't loan it to him, unless you can give it to him. Give without thought of getting back. When you do that, you've transferred the man's debt from him to God! And God always pays his debts.

The Bible also says, *"If you lend to those from whom you expect repayment, what credit is that to you? Even 'sinners' lend to 'sinners' expecting to be repaid in full."* Rather, *"lend to them without expecting to get anything back. Then your reward will be great, and you will be sons of the Most High."* 4

Some will be repaid to you here on earth. Some will be repaid in heaven. (By the way, if you aren't sure you are going to heaven, get yourself a Bible and read the Gospel according to St. Mark)

It may sound a little strange that in a book that is entitled "How To Keep More of What You Make!" the first thing I tell you to do is to give it away, but this principle is so key to everything else in the book, I want you to get it right away.

Give it ALL away?

Okay, that's a little extreme. I'm not talking about giving away everything you own. But by taking the first part of your income and giving a portion of it away, you are saying in effect, "the rest of the money doesn't have an unnatural hold on me, it doesn't own me, I don't own it, I'm simply the steward of the stuff."

Giving away a portion of your money sets the right tone, and triggers the second part of the principle, which is *"...it will be given to you. A good measure, pressed down, shaken together and running over, will be poured into your lap. For with the measure you use, it will be measured out to you!"*5 This means that when you do your part (giving) you will begin receiving even more than what you gave. Don't get me wrong or put any words in my mouth now. There's no dollar for dollar exchange rate, and you may not see it come in as dollars at all, but things will happen. Winter coats go on sale just as your old coat falls apart. An unexpected refund check comes in from your insurance carrier. You leave a bag of presents and Christmas dinner on the doorstep of a hurting family, and enjoy the rest of the holidays on the feeling you receive.

No government program can equal the power of an individual giving his own money to another person. One hundred percent of your gift gets to the intended recipient. No one deducts overhead expenses, nothing is taken out for marketing costs, administration, mailings or anything else. All of it goes where it is needed most. Best of all, you decide who gets it, and why.

Every day you will be bombarded by a thousand opportunities to give. Some are legitimate, others are scoundrels that take advantage of generous people. Here are a couple of tips on giving:

- ***Be wise in who and what you give to.*** Checkout the organizations you give to. Make sure they are legitimate charities, and that most of what you give actually goes towards their stated goals. Some so-called charities suck up 90% of donations for 'administrative' costs.
- ***Decide what you can afford to give in advance.*** Settle on a monthly budget of what you can give, and stick to it. Don't allow emotional appeals to increase your giving, there-by forcing you to short change other budget items.
- ***Giving doesn't have to be in dollars.*** Look for chances to give, not only of your money, but of your time, as well. Your time and talents may be more appreciated than your dollars in some situations.

For Christians Only

I'm going to step aside briefly and take a moment with my Christian brothers and sisters. If you don't see your self in that way you can jump ahead to the next chapter starting on page 39, or listen in, it's alright.

I'd like to say a word here about the tithe. The word "tithe" literally means one tenth. Tithing a tithe means giving ten percent of your income, off the top, before paying anything else. More important than the percentage, however, is your heart attitude towards your money, and towards God. By being faithful with the tithe, you are placing your financial situation under the authority of God.

The Old Testament records Abraham giving a tenth of all he had as a tithe to the Lord.[6] The mosaic law commanded the children of Israel to give one tenth of all that they had as a tithe to God.[7] Malachi even went so far as to accuse the Israelites of stealing from God, how? By not paying the tithe.[8]

However, today, many Christians are quick to point out that there is no such specific command to "tithe" in the New Testament. They argue that God has left the matter entirely up to us to decide. You can tithe if you want to, or not, as you decide. As a result, only a small percentage of Christians tithe today. According to the Barna Research Group only eight percent of American Christians tithe.[9]

This is an important matter, and I don't think it's that complicated. I believe that Christ didn't spell out a command to tithe, because the Christian life is to be lived by faith, grace and liberty, not by the strictness of the law. However, Christ said that he came to fulfill the law, not destroy it. The principles laid down in the law are still in effect today. The ten commandments are for us, just as much as they were for Israel. The difference is that our salvation is not based upon keeping rules, but upon the blood of Christ shed on the cross. Even though Christ fulfilled the law of Moses, and, therefore the tithe isn't a condition of salvation, it is still a sound financial principle that God wants us to take advantage of. Remember, the tithe pre-dated the law of Moses. Before the law was given, Abraham showed his devotion to God by giving a tenth of all he had.

Unfortunately, for many, tithing represents a huge burden on their finances, and an even larger leap of faith. They say to the Lord, "I don't have enough to pay all of my bills now, with out tithing, how can I pay them all and tithe?" How do I know this? Because its exactly what I said to him.

Let me tell you the story of the five pennies. It was the mid-eighties, and my family and I weren't doing too well financially. My husband had been laid off and our two income family was down to one. We were thousands of dollars in debt, and were in danger of losing our home. Every month we sold something else to pay our mortgage. Every month our finances got worse and worse.

Even though I knew I should be tithing, I didn't have the faith to give. I couldn't see how giving away part of our meager income would help. Yet, at the same time, I wanted to be obedient to God, and the matter of giving the tithe was always on my heart.

"God, you know I can't afford to give ten percent right now." I told him.

"How about five pennies." He answered, impressing my heart with the idea. "Can you afford five pennies?"

I knew I could come up with five cents. I began giving a "tithe" of only five pennies. I know five cents was not literally ten percent of our income, but God met me where my faith was, and began to teach me and develop in me a trust for him. After a few weeks, he challenged me to making it five nickels. I thought we could afford five nickels, so I bumped it up. A little later he suggested five dimes, then five quarters, and eventually five one-dollar bills. At every new step, I knew I could make the leap, and God was honoring my faith, as small as it was.

Finally, he came to me and said, "How about five five-dollar bills?" I admit I had to think about that one. Twenty-five dollars a week was a lot in 1985, but we started giving five five-dollar bills.

Throughout this time God showed his faithfulness to me and my family. Little by little supernatural things began to happen. We were able to get out of the house we were in and get into a home that was perfect for us. Our new neighborhood was a delight. Instead of payments that were choking us, we had a home we could afford on one income. Our new neighbors were Christians, on one side lived the Churches, and across the street lived the Miracles. I felt that God hand picked the home and the neighbors for us.

He began to show me inventive ways to make the money stretch. He helped me sell furniture I'd found for free. I had an old car I was trying to get rid of. I wound up selling the parts of it for more than the car was worth. In the end someone even paid me thirty-five dollars for the body as scrap metal. Things I needed were given to me. Blessings came rolling in. For instance, I love shutters, and my new home had none, but, I got all I needed when a neighbor remodeled and scrapped all of theirs.

The point is, in the times of my life when I did not tithe, my finances were not healthy. When I am faithful with the tithe, my finances are much better. God wants us to tithe so that we can exercise our faith in him, and He can unleash his blessings in our lives. I encourage you to pray about it, and if you are not tithing right now, unleash this powerful tool in your life.

Making the leap

So, now that you've decided to take God up on his challenge to tithe, how do you do it? Do you pay all of your other bills and then see what's left over? Or do you just close your eyes and write the check, without a thought for your bills?

Let's see what the Bible has to say about it. King Solomon, a man noted for his extraordinary wisdom, wrote: "*Honor the Lord with your wealth, with the firstfruits of all your crops; then your barns will be filled to overflowing and your vats will brim over with new wine.*"[10] This verse instructs us to give the first ten percent of our income. I believe what God is saying is: "Take it off the top, before you know whether or not you think you can afford it."

Where is the faith in figuring out how much you can afford prior to giving the tithe? There isn't any. It takes no faith at all to go through your finances, figure what you can squeeze by on, and pay the rest for a tithe. That's just like the rich men Jesus saw in the temple giving out of their abundance. Yet the one Jesus called our attention to was the little woman who dropped in just two cents. He said to his disciples that she had given more than all of the rest combined, since they gave only from their excess, and she gave all she had.[11]

I believe God wants us to give before we know how much we can afford. That's the ideal. That's where he wants us to be. That's also where the greatest blessings are. But, just like he met me where I was in my faith, he will meet you. Put God first and he will begin to bless you.

He also wants you to give what you give in joy. *"...for God loves a cheerful giver."*[12] Said St. Paul in his second letter to the Corinthian church. Let your attitude in giving be one of cheerful worship. You have the privilege of helping do the work of the Lord. God doesn't want your tithes and offerings if you are giving out of a sense of guilt, greed or condemnation. He wants you to give out of your worship and faith. He also promised that when you gave, he would give.

St. Paul viewed your giving as the 'seeds' you sow for harvest. He said *"Remember this: Whoever sows sparingly will also reap sparingly, and whoever sows generously will also reap generously. Each man should give what he has decided in his heart to give, not reluctantly or under compulsion, for God loves a cheerful giver. And God is able to make all grace abound to you, so that in all things at all times, having all that you need, you will abound in every good work. As it is written: 'He has scattered abroad his gifts to the poor; his righteousness endures forever.' Now he who supplies seed to the sower and bread for food will also supply and increase your store of seed and will enlarge the harvest of your righteousness. You will be made rich in every way so that you can be generous on every occasion, and through us your generosity will result in thanksgiving to God."*[13]

Did you catch that? God wants us to be cheerful givers so that He can trust us with more so that we can give more. "*You will be made rich in every way so that you can be generous on every occasion, and through us your generosity will result in thanksgiving to God."*[14]

So, what have we learned? God wants us to give cheerfully, right off the top, and give what we decide we can give. Hey, that could easily be MORE than ten percent!

Ok, that's it, no more insider stuff.

GET (AND KEEP) A JOB

You know, maybe before we start with the tips on saving money, I should say word about making money. I only include this because I see so many people in dead-end jobs that they hate wishing they had better jobs.

Know what you want.

"Know yourself," the philosopher said. Many people are working where they work by accident. They took the first job offered them whether or not the work suited them. Take the time to imagine what your perfect job would be like, and then only go after that kind of job.

Do what you love.

When you like what you do, you will be more effective and make more money. I've run into so many people who hate their work. They hate the boss, the customers, and the work they do. It's little wonder that they make no success out of it. What a terrible way to live. Yet, we are told that 'you've got to do the things you don't like in order to do the things you do like.' What a crock of number one grade-A bull chips. No one has chained you to your current job. Get the training you need to change careers and go for it!

If you can't do what you love, love what you do.

Sometimes, you can't just quit the current job, and you have to suck it up. You're still in luck. Your attitude is the most important factor whether or not you will hate your job. It is possible to take a job you hate and make it a job you love by simply making a choice. You can choose to be happy, at least until you have made a way to leave your current job.

Stay on the cutting edge.

Nearly every field in American commerce has radically changed in the last fifteen years. At one time in America, a college degree served a person his entire business career. Now, new advances come upon the heals of discoveries upon inventions so fast that a person must continually fight to keep current. Read the journals of your industry. Go back to night school to get the credentials you need for that next promotion. Stay on top of new technology and terminology.

Be a pleasant person to work with.

Honey catches more flies than vinegar. You don't want be a doormat, or a 'yes-man,' of course, but don't be the company whiner either.

Be diligent in your work.

I know you do the very best at all times for your employer or your customers. However, there are other slackers out there who need to hear this: Get back to work!

Keep your value high.

Your company buys your labor, knowledge and judgment from you and sells it to their customers. If your contribution becomes too expensive relative to its value, or your value drops below your selling point, your company will ultimately stop buying from you, and find a more economical source. On the other hand, if the value of your work is higher than the amount your company pays for it, you have a much-improved bargaining position for getting better compensation.

Have a plan for layoffs.

Sooner or later almost everyone loses his or her position. Having a plan in place for surviving a layoff protects your family during the transition, and leaves you free to concentrate on landing your next job. Your plan should include:

- ***A savings safety net.*** This should be enough to cover the difference between your monthly bills and your expected unemployment payments. This safety net must be in place prior to the layoff.
- ***Notification to your debtors*** that you have been laid off and a request for reduced payments during the layoff period. This will at least keep them informed, and delay any formal action against you should you fall behind.
- ***A comprehensive plan*** of attack to locate and obtain a new job. (This is the subject of an entire book, and we won't attempt to cover it here.)

How To Keep More of What you Make!

I LOVE IT PERKINS! WE COLLECT MORE THAN THEY OWE EVERY MONTH. WE KEEP IT ALL YEAR INTEREST FREE, AND THEY'RE HAPPY TO GET A REFUND EVERY APRIL 15TH!
IRS.

Excess withholdings are really interest free loans to the IRS.

"I'm proud to be paying taxes in the United States. The only thing is I could be just as proud for half the money."

Arthur Godfrey

THE TAX MAN COMETH

Having laid the ground rules lets move on to the specific practical things you can do to save more of what you make.

We have already established that since money represents your time, labor and energy, you have the right to save as much as your own money as possible to use as you see fit.

However, there are those who believe they can spend your money much more effectively than you can. We call these people government bureaucrats. As it stands today, taxation represents the biggest loss to most people's income. Depending on your income bracket, your paycheck, your dividends, your interest, rent receipts, and even your baby-sitting money is subject to between ten and thirty-eight percent taxation.

If you don't mind this, you may be a Democrat. If you are philosophically opposed to this, odds are, you may be a Republican, or a Libertarian. If you try to avoid paying taxes, you are just plain human. Even the most prominent Democrats try to reduce their tax burdens. No doubt, you have heard of former President Clinton's tax return in which the first family valued their donated underwear at \$2.50 per piece. This amounts to a tax savings of \$.96 for each set of briefs!

According to the Tax Foundation, the average American family worked until April 27 to pay off all the taxes levied on them through out the year 2002. The Tax Foundation coined the term "Tax Freedom Day" as the day upon which this event occurs. In Washington State, the date was actually May 9, to account for our state's higher taxes. This may seem incredulous to you, but remember, included are property taxes, sales taxes, gas taxes, state and federal income taxes, estate taxes, excise taxes and motor vehicle taxes. It also includes a host of other fees that we don't realize are taxes: building permits, marriage licenses, drivers licenses, user fees and so many more, it makes me mad to sit here and try to think of them.

So what can you do? Well the Supreme Court has ruled that you have the right to ***AVOID*** taxes, as long as you do not ***EVADE*** them. What's the difference? When you avoid taxes, you take steps to reduce your tax burden by legally investing in tax-free mutual funds, or writing off your home interest, or buying a car in a city with a lower sales tax rate. Evading taxes is what happens when you report less than what you actually earned, or inflate your deductions.

Here are some tips on avoiding taxes:

- ***Buy a home.*** If you want the secret to saving thousands of dollars at tax time, buy your own home. Every dollar and dime you spend on your home mortgage interest is totally tax deductible up to the value of the home. The current personal deduction allowed by the IRS is $7850 for a married couple filing jointly. That means that every American married couple has the right to deduct $7850 off their 2002 taxes, without itemizing a thing. This is great news if you are not a homeowner, and don't have very much in the way of work related deductions to make. If however, you have ever agonized over the fact that your itemized deductions were just barely enough to use, then buying a home is for you. Today's average yearly interest payments on a home well exceed $7850. Thus, you may now deduct all of your other deductions, charitable gifts and losses from your taxable income.

- ***Convert your credit card debt to home equity debt.*** In addition to getting a better interest rate and a lower payment (in most cases), you will be allowed to deduct all of your interest (up to the value of the house) from your taxes. WARNING: Don't use your home equity to pay credit card debt without closing the credit cards. Too many people transfer their credit card debt, and then max out their cards again, putting them in a worse position than before.

- ***Be careful where you buy your clothes and big-ticket items.*** Find out which of the local municipalities has the lowest sales tax, and shop there if possible (just don't spend more in gas than you save in sales tax).
    - For example: my husband and I found a furniture store in Lynnwood that had a location in Everett. We purchased the furniture in the Lynnwood store but had it delivered to the Everett store, because the sales tax was lower in Everett. Washington state sales tax is levied at the point of delivery.

- ***Be careful where you buy a car.*** Some cities impose a Motor Vehicle Excise Tax (MVET) in addition to the state MVET; don't buy a car in those places. Alternatively, negotiate the cost of the city

MVET off the price of the car by pointing out to the salesperson you could just go down the road and buy a car in a different city. Seattle has a Monorail MVET of 1.4%. However it is only levied on residents of Seattle upon the first anniversary of the purchase of the car.

- ***Be a shrewd shopper.*** If a neighboring community has a lower sales tax rate, shop there. Just keep an eye on the retail prices are the same or lower than those in around your home.
- ***When looking at homes to buy, check into the local property taxes.*** Be aware of what you will be paying year after year. Does the city or county government have a history of frequently raising

local property taxes? If so, they are likely to continue to do so.

- ***Don't send the IRS more money than they need.*** Reduce the amount withheld from your paycheck every week. Claim the maximum amount of deductions that will allow you to pay just what is necessary in taxes. Why send Washington thousands of dollars that you don't owe? They will keep your money all year, pay you no interest on it and then make it seem like they are doing you a favor to send a portion of it back to you. Figure your exemptions carefully, for underpayment of taxes carries a penalty. Take that extra money and put it to work for you. Even if you only put it into a savings account you'll get a better return than letting the IRS hold on to it for you, interest free.

- ***Plan your estate.*** Good estate planning will help you preserve what you have saved for your family when you die. It starts with a will, but it certainly doesn't stop there. If you die without a will, your estate will most likely pay a lot more taxes than necessary. I'm not an estate planner, so I won't try to give you specific advice here. Just find a planner you can trust, and take care of this important issue.

YOU BET YOUR LIFE INSURANCE

Every month you make a series of bets with one or more insurance companies. You make a bet that you are going to die this month. If you are wrong, you pay the life insurance company a small amount, say $40. If you are right, they pay your estate a large amount, say $500,000.

You bet the car insurance company that you will get into an accident this month, the medical insurance company that you will get sick and the homeowners company that you'll have a fire. It's the only time you feel good about loosing a bet. The real gamble, however, is not placing the bets! By paying out a little every month, we try to control the unexpected disasters of life, and avoid their devastating effects.

The danger is that you can easily spend much more than you need to every month. That cuts into your savings, reduces your effective income and puts off your goals a little longer. Try these strategies for keeping your insurance premiums as low as possible, without exposing yourself to undue risk.

- ***Get volume discounts on insurance.*** Many companies offer discounts when you insure your home and car with them, or insure multiple vehicles under the same policy.
- ***Shop around!*** Make sure you are getting the best price for your money. Insurance rates vary wildly, don't just take the first quote you are given.

- ***Balance cost with service.*** Beware of buying cheep insurance over the internet. Dealing directly with an insurance company can save you money, but it can also leave you without an advocate if the time comes to make a claim. Having a local broker who is looking out for you, and knows the intricacies of dealing with the claims adjusters is a real value.
- ***Buy only the insurance you really need.*** Know what your insurance covers, and only cover the things you can't reasonably pay for yourself. For instance, don't carry full-coverage on your second car if it's a beater since it's value is probably lower than the deductible.
- ***Don't always buy insurance when renting a car.*** Check to see if you car insurance will cover a damaged rental. If it does include rentals, decide whether or not you need to pay additional insurance at the rental counter.
- ***Do buy insurance when renting small equipment.*** Usually, the value of equipment you rent is less than the deductible on your homeowner's or renter's insurance. The few dollars extra to insure the item with the rental store can really save you money if you happen to damage it in use.
- ***Carry larger deductibles.*** The difference between premiums for low deductible polices and those of high deductible policies can be amazing. If you are worried about paying higher deductibles, take the difference in the premiums each month, and drop it in a savings account, until you have enough to cover your deductible. From then on, the difference in the premiums can go to other important items.

How To Keep More of What you Make!

- ***Get credit for your safety devices.*** Make sure your auto carrier credits you for anti-lock brakes, air bags and passive restraint systems. Additionally, most give you credits for alarm systems and for buying certain makes and models.
- ***Become a shareholder.*** You may be eligible through work or a family member to join a non-profit insurance company that is owned by it's shareholders. One such company is USAA. Members must have served or have a family member who has served in the U.S. military. Each year you will receive your share of the excess premiums, often $80-120!
- ***Drive safely.*** Your behavior behind the wheel has a direct effect on your premiums. Fines for speeding or drunk driving are only the beginning of your expenses. Your insurance carrier has the right to raise your rates, or refuse to insure you altogether.

There are worse things in life than death. Have you ever spent an evening with an insurance salesman?
Woody Allen

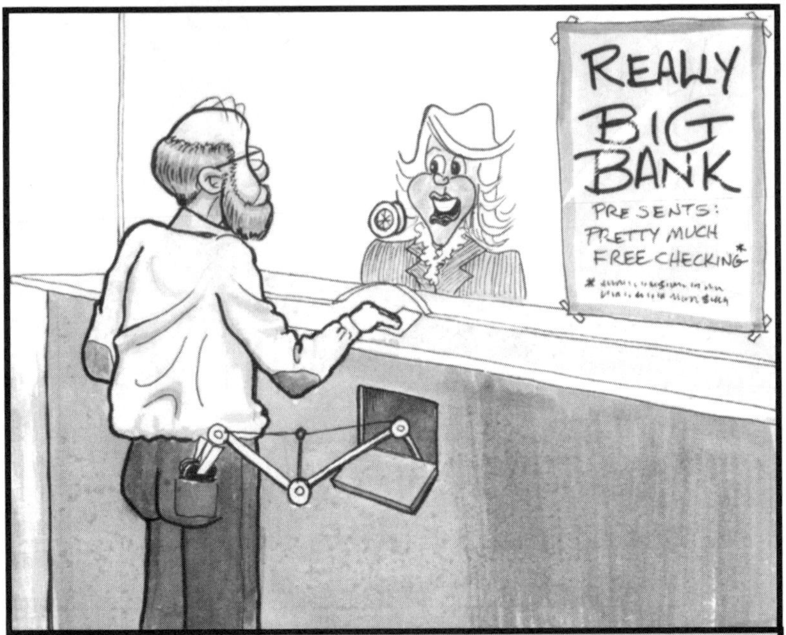

"Is your checking really free?"
"Yes Sir! It's absolutely, positively pretty-much free!"

Show me a man with really free checking, and I'll show you a guy who hasn't read the fine print!

BREAKING THE BANK

Here's another place where complacency can cost you. Banks actively look for new fees to charge you. Be aware of what your bank is charging you. Is your checking really free? Or is it free only if you behave yourself, don't make any mistakes, and use less than ten checks per month? What kind of strategies are there for minimizing the costs of banking? Well that's what we're here for, isn't it!

- ***Again, shop around!*** Find the best account that fits your needs for the least amount of money. Look for free checking accounts. Realize however, that many banks *CLAIM* to have free checking, but then add fees in the fine print. Some banks offer free checking, but not free checks. Others offer both. Investigate the costs of banking online compared to a free checking account. Often banks will offer either or.
- ***Look at your total financial picture*** when choosing a bank. What do you need. Are you just interested in an checking account? Are you looking for the best rates on short and long term CD's? Do you want a bank that also offers investment securities? Compare account costs verses savings rates, especially on things such as 30 day CD's, savings interest rates, 6 month CD's. etc. Can you afford to keep a minimum balance in a free checking account if it isn't earning you money?

How To Keep More of What you Make!

- ***Use money orders.*** If you are paying debt collectors, always use money orders to keep your account information private. Make sure your bank offers free money orders.
- ***Do NOT bounce checks.*** I once worked with a person who turned a two dollar check into two hundred dollars worth of returned check fees, collection fees and interest. Keep your checking account accurate by entering every check as you write it, and using a calculator to keep your figures right. As an alternative to the old checkbook, there are very good home accounting programs available to track your checking, savings, investments and loans from your home computer. What ever method you use, use it regularly.
- ***Control your debit cards.*** Debit cards have made it easier than ever before to directly access your checking account. However, they also present a grave danger in the form of lost receipts and forgotten transactions. Unless you record your debit card transactions with the same diligence as your checks, you run the risk of over-extending yourself. If you are personally unable to keep your card in your wallet, then leave it at home! In fact, try this for one month: Both you and your spouse put your debit cards in an envelope tucked away in your file cabinet. Agree with each other that neither will touch the cards for one month unless both agree on the use. Then, when your next statement comes in compare it with last month's statement and see how much money you saved!
- ***Need something notarized?*** Your bank usually will do it for free. Find out what other services they offer for free.

- ***Get the best rate!*** Does the interest rate on your credit card reflect your good credit? Time and time again I find that people with outstanding credit scores, anything 700 and above, are still paying 19 – 24% interest on their credit cards! That can chew up a lot of money! Call the card's issuing bank and tell them you will close the account if they don't give you a much better rate. If they don't drop your rate, switch to a one that has the rate you want.
- ***Pay off your balance monthly.*** Use a card that waives interest on any balance paid within 30 days, and keep it paid off. This will force you to keep your credit transactions to the bare minimum, and it will save you hundreds of dollars in interest fees every year.
- ***Get a line of credit instead of credit cards.*** If you can qualify for a line of credit with your bank or credit union, it will usually offer you a much better interest rate than credit cards. Because you must actually transfer an amount from your line of credit to your checking account to spend the money, it's psychologically more difficult to spend the money frivolously. Make it a policy to pay down the line of credit above and beyond the regular monthly payment.
- ***Keep a rainy day fund.*** Putting aside $500 to $1000 in an emergency fund can help smooth out the unexpected bumps in the road. Many financial advisors tell you to keep two to three months salary in the bank. If you can do that, great! At the minimum you should have enough to cover a major car repair, and the deductibles on your auto, home owner's, and health insurances combined. Build up this emergency buffer by saving $50 to $100 per

month. Have an understanding with your spouse that this money can only be used for emergencies. Sorry guys, boat fever is not considered life threatening.

- ***Pay yourself first.*** Or second, if you have decided to begin tithing. Set aside ten percent of your income to save toward your goals. Do this before you start paying the bills. I know this is counter-intuitive. I know you've been taught to pay the bills first and save what ever is left over. The problem with that scenario is that often, what's left over doesn't seem worth saving. So, put ten percent into your savings account. Then pay the bills. If you absolutely must, you can withdraw just enough to cover the bills. But leave the rest, no matter how small in the savings account. Remember, this is one of the reasons you are learning to be a penny pincher. This is a major principle. It's simple to say, but hard to do. Pay your self first.

SAVING ON UTILITIES

Utility bills are great places to save extra money. Hardly anyone bothers to examine a phone bill, question the charges or have them removed. Utility bills come regularly every month, they remain about the same every month, and so they lull you to sleep with the idea that "Oh, I'm just the electric bill. There's nothing you can do about me." Well, it's time to take that little sucker by the throat and shake your dollars out! Here's how:

- ***Electricity on the budget plan.*** Your power company may give you a choice in paying your electric bill. Some power companies bill you once every two months for your actual usage. This can be staggering depending on the season. Check to see if they offer an annualized budget plan. The budget plan gives you a single monthly amount that doesn't change with the seasons. This makes budgeting a lot easier. You'll be saving up for the winter in the summer months, and avoid heart wrenching surprises in December.
- ***Insulate your electric hot water tank.*** If it is an older model, wrap it with an insulation blanket, or consider replacing it with a more fuel-efficient and better-insulated model. Do this BEFORE it springs a leak and ruins everything in your basement or garage. **Warning:** Never wrap a gas or oil hot water tank. This could interfere with the air intake, resulting in inefficient combustion, and wasted fuel.

How To Keep More of What you Make!

- ***Convert your hot water heater.*** Heating water burns up more electricity than any other appliance you have. If you have gas or oil available to you, convert your water tank and save! Also, fix any leaks in the hot water lines, or the faucets. In addition to saving costly repairs to your home, it will save you a lot of money on the electric bill.

- ***Kill your baseboard heaters.*** Baseboard heat is the only thing that uses more electricity than an electric water tank. If you have gas available on your street, call your gas company for a free estimate on installing a new gas furnace. Today's gas furnaces convert up to 90% of the fuel's energy into usable heat for your home. You can usually get a reduced rate loan to cover the cost of conversion.

- ***No gas? go for oil or propane instead.*** If you don't have gas, and the gas company isn't planning on providing service to your neighborhood any time soon, then install oil or propane. Even in areas of the country where electricity is relatively cheap, oil, gas or propane will save you money.

- ***Use your dryer and stove as a heat source when in use.*** Vent your dryer into the house to provide extra heat when in use. Place nylon over the vent to trap the lint. Take care to clean this with each use to keep your dryer running safely. While baking, set a fan up to move air out of the kitchen and into other parts of the house. This will keep your kitchen much cooler while helping to heat your home.

- ***Maximize cooking energy.*** When using the oven, try to cook multiple dishes at once to conserve energy.

- ***Pickup FREE fuel.*** Keep an eye out for classified ads and signs that advertise free firewood. Just make sure you observe the burn bans. There is no sense saving money on fuel to spend it on tickets.
- ***Replace the furnace air filters*** regularly to improve airflow and reduce wear on the blower unit. Also, have the system vacuumed out at least once every three years to reduce dust build up.
- ***Is your water metered?*** Some homeowners have water meters instead of paying a flat fee. If yours is metered, don't pass up the opportunity to save on this often over looked bill. Put flow restrictors in all of your faucets, (this is required by law for new construction or remodeling) fix leaky faucets, and singing toilets. Catch leaking toilets by dropping red food dye into the tank. Don't flush the tank. If the dye seeps into the bowl, you have a leak that is costing you money.
- ***Learn to recycle effectively.*** Recycling can reduce the volume of your garbage by a third or more. Thus, if you were setting out three cans of garbage, by recycling, you will reduce your garbage bill by one can per week.
- ***Make your cell phone plan fit your needs!*** Cell phone and pager companies have widely different plans. Compare them for value and service. Find the plan that best suits your needs. Stick with the basic plans that don't charge for unnecessary frills.
- ***Be careful of family plan cell phone deals.*** Often you can add an additional phone to your primary service for a nominal fee: ten bucks or so per month. However, each phone is using up the same 600 or 800 minutes per month. Make sure you both

can keep within the limits of the plan. Extra minutes are costly! Generally, two separate cell phone plans will be worth the extra cost. You'll both get the number of minutes you need, and your phone bills will be stable.

- ***Check your telephone bills for inaccuracies.*** Make sure you know the numbers called. Contest charges to phone numbers you don't recognize.
- ***Challenge 900 number calls.*** If you have a minor in the house that has made some 900 number calls, you may have them removed, one time. Then you will have to deal with the person making the calls. This only applies if the caller was a minor.
- ***Reduce your cable bill by removing the premium movie channels.*** Most libraries now carry extensive stocks of videos, and most video rentals have specials to bring in people on 'off' nights of the week.
- ***Monitor your usage.*** Keep a log book of how much you are using the premium channels. Is it worth the cost? You may be surprised at how much time you spend in front of the TV.

Faith is like electricity. You can't see it, but you can see the light.

Author Unknown

New member? No, Mr. Max has been a member since 1997. This is his annual New Year's Resolution Visit!

THE GYM

Americans love health clubs. We buy memberships, we buy fancy workout togs, we resolve to lose weight, gain muscle, look better and feel better. Then before January has turned the corner, we're back on the couch watching professional athletes exercise for a living. Come on America! Get off your duff! Get out the sweat socks and headbands. Grab your Gatorade and let's go!

- ***Be sure the gym you are using is getting full use.*** Don't let your membership sit while you get out of shape. Most memberships cost between forty and sixty dollars per month. That's $480 to $720 per year! If you aren't going to use the gym, then, at least cancel that expense. Keep the gym and use it to it's maximum potential. You'll feel better and be in great shape for the summer garage sales!

- ***Use the landlord's stuff.*** Does your apartment or condominium have an exercise room available to you? Take advantage of it. You'll get to meet your neighbors and save money and work out all at the same time! But don't talk to the cute redhead, your spouse won't like that.

- ***If you can't afford the gym, improvise.*** Take the dog for a walk. You'll both love it. Track how far you walk each day. Buy a swim pass at the local pool. Park at the far end of parking lots and walk. Take the stairs instead of the elevator. Do lots of push-backs. What's a push-back? It's like a push-up, except you do it while sitting at the dinner table.

Place your hands firmly on the edge of the table, and push back until your plate is out of reach.

- ***Don't purchase exercise equipment*** for your home unless you already use that same equipment in the gym. This will ensure your home equipment does not wind up as a clothes rack. This especially applies to equipment sold via TV infomercials. A lot of these are simply over priced gimmicks that just don't work.
- ***Shop the used market.*** If you are going to buy equipment for the home, check out the garage sales, thrift shops, second hand stores and pawn shops first. A lot of what you'll find has hardly been used, except as clothes racks or abstract sculptures.

HOUSEHOLD PURCHASING

Saving money when you are spending it is an art. First, don't get suckered into buying something you had no intention of buying just because you saw it on sale. This is called impulse buying, and it's bad. It's great for the guy who just sold you his last purple alligator clock with built in sushi timer, but if you didn't intend to buy such a thing when you left home, you haven't saved money, you've lost it. Besides, where you putting that thing? It's purple! Ugh. Secondly, *do* watch the sales. Obviously you want to buy for less money. Just be sure the sales really are sales, and not reduced prices off of ridiculously high starting prices, in other words, watch the market.

- ***Get on and stay on a budget.*** Oh, I know, everyone hates living on a budget, but this is probably the number one remedy for most financial troubles. A budget will help you see where you are now, and help monitor your progress as you reach your goals. There are hundreds of books on the market that will teach you how to budget effectively, so I won't go into more detail here. Even if all you do is list all your expenses and subtract them from your income, you'll have a clearer picture of your actual financial situation.

- ***Wait for it.*** When purchasing big-ticket items, wait and watch the sales. Call around for the best prices, and do your home work. You can save hundreds of dollars by being aware of the market. This also gives you a cooling down period between the first breathless time you see that 54" wide screen TV with automatic pre-pixel post-modulation, and the time you actually plunk down the cash, to say to your self: "Can I really afford to spend three thousand dollars on a TV set?" If during the waiting period you decide that yes, you will spend the price of a small used car to bring the great sport of curling to your living room in all it's broom swishing glory, then at least, you will have found the best deal. Do your home work. Wait and research. Watch and save.

- ***Six Months Same As Cash!*** Only take advantage of 'six-months-same-as-cash' deals if you can pay these off in the six month time frame. If you don't pay off the amount within the agreed time frame, you will owe all the financing charges. These deals usually carry an interest rate of 24.99%. Move the debt to a lower rate card if you can. If you have the discipline to pay off the amount within the 90, 180 or 360 days of the plan, and this is not an impulse buy, and you really can't wait to save the amount and then buy it, then, well, okay.

- ***Never, never impulse buy!*** Here are the warning signs of an impending impulse purchase:
    - You didn't leave home looking for it.
    - It's on sale.
    - You can buy it six-months-same-as-cash.
    - It's red.
    - It's really, really cool!
    - You can't think of an actual use for it.
    - It's chocolate.
    - It was sitting at or near the front counter.
    - You would have to sneak it past your spouse.

- The store manager drools a little while you stare at it.

Impulse buying makes it impossible to keep to a budget. Coincidentally, budgets severely curtail impulse buying. If you really want to keep more of what you make, you must master this issue. Many people pickup an candy bar at the store, or a magazine, or other such small ticket items. You may think that it's no big deal, but even these small transactions add up to a huge hit to the monthly budget. Other people go shopping with no clear idea of what they are looking for, and come back with boxes of over priced clothes, gadgets and stuff that has no real value. Here's one of the worst examples of impulse buying I've heard of: my friend went back to the office to do some extra work one evening, but never got there. Instead, on a whim, he stopped in and purchased a used car, totally unprepared and un-researched. He later told me it was the worst auto purchase he'd ever made.

- ***Use Resale shops and garage sales*** to shop for clothing, appliances, furniture, or anything else of value. Don't you love garage sales? I do. You never know what you will find, and there's always the hope that somewhere out there is an undiscovered Picasso that granny stuck up in the attic because it was too 'weird' for her. But the real value of thrift stores, second hand shops, pawn shops and garage sales is the opportunity to find quality used items you need for much less than their new retail cost. If you're the type of person who would never dream of wearing used clothing, I'd like to point out that everything in your closet is used.

I have a friend who's children all wore great Disney outfits on their vacation to the happiest place on earth, each with the Disney logo and Disney characters, but without the Disney price. These togs were picked up for pennies on the dollar at local thrift stores, and the savings helped pay for the trip. No one asked if their clothes had come from Disneyland, or thrifty-land.

- ***When buying at thrift stores, be picky, picky, picky.*** Inspect everything. Search out the good stuff. You'll find business suits, casual wear, exercise outfits, work rags, and mountains of great kid's clothes. It's not all out in the open however. You have to go looking for it. They're tucked away like gems in the gravel of a stream bed. You have to sift through the lime green leisure suits and the shocking pink spandex workout shorts to find them, but they are there. Good luck, and good hunting!
- ***Buy in bulk, and save.*** Whether it's a ten pound bag of rice, a thirty six pack of toilet paper, or a fifty pound bag of dog food, buying in bulk saves you more than buying smaller quantities. If you have a discount club card like Costco or Price Saver's, or Sam's Club, (or know someone who does) you may be able to save quite a bit from your grocery bills by purchasing long shelf life items in bulk. Don't be afraid to buy the big cans of ketchup or other liquids and pastes. Just keep a couple of regular sized containers and refill them.

My dog is worried about the economy because Alpo is up to 99 cents a can. That's almost $7.00 in dog money.

Joe Weinstein

Dude! Check it out, I found this place that totally rents videos for FREE! It's called... "the Library."

THAT'S ENTERTAINMENT

It could be argued that Americans spend too much on entertainment. In the year 2000, for instance, Americans spent more money to see that year's top summer blockbuster movie, ***Mission Impossible 2***, than the combined amount spent by both major campaigns for president. This seems like the perfect place to save some money. Now, don't get me wrong. I enjoy a good movie just as much as anyone, and I know how important it is to blow off steam every once in a while, but if you are trying to save money for a specific goal, or to get past a lean time at work, this is a non-essential that can be drastically cut. What I'm going to show you is how to save money and still enjoy yourself.

- ***Wait for the video.*** Admit it. Most movies don't need to be seen on the big screen. Maybe you guys out there will argue that big explosions must be seen on big screens to be fully appreciated, but for the most part, waiting to watch a movie until it comes out on video is no big deal. Most movies move from theater release to video in less than six months now. Of course, the better the movie, the longer the wait. The record holder for fastest time from big screen to TV screen (for a "major blockbuster") must have been Mathew Broderick's, stinkeroo, ***Godzilla.*** Wow, what a skunk cabbage! Glad I didn't spend eight bucks on it!

- ***Get Free entertainment!*** Music CD's, videos, and DVD's may all be borrowed from your local library for FREE! In addition to today's hits, you'll find a wide selection of classic movies, foreign films, children's movies, musicals, mysteries, dramas, comedies, and documentaries. You'll get jazz and reggae, rock and rock-a-billy, classical and new age. All this for the price of a library card; still free in most places.

- ***Compare rental prices.*** Okay, the library doesn't have the very latest video releases. That doesn't mean you should pay full price for rentals. The major video chain stores charge almost four bucks for a new release! Our local grocery store rents all their videos for $.79 on Monday nights. Combined with their 3-for-a-dollar candy specials, you've got an entire family night at the movies for less than five bucks! Watch for "rent 3 get one free" specials, or 3- for-3-for-3 sales (three videos for three days for three bucks).

- ***Buy them cheep.*** Thrift shops, second hand stores, and pawn shops all buy and sell videos, DVD's, CD's and video games. Just make sure you can return it if it doesn't work.

- ***Read to your children.*** While you're at the library for videos, stop by and reacquaint yourself with Dr. Seuss, E.B. White, and Robert Lewis Stevenson. You'll have a great time with the kids, and instill a love for reading that will carry on for the rest of their lives. Read the book their favorite movie was based upon. Talk about the differences and similarities between the movie and the book. Have them imagine how they would have made the movie differently.

- ***Turn the TV OFF!*** Make it game night, instead of movie night! Pull out all the old favorites, and have a blast. Don't have any board games? Thrift shops are a great source of inexpensive board games. You can buy lots of yesterday's top board games for just a couple of bucks! Just make sure all the pieces are there!

HEALTH AND MEDICAL

What ever your source of medical coverage, whether you have major medical through work, have a state sponsored medical program, or you simply pay out of pocket, you pay some part of your medical bills, some or all of your insurance premiums, and part or all of your prescription medicines. Many people believe that there is nothing you can do as a consumer to reduce your medical bills. Here are some tips on keeping costs down and challenging costs you may not owe.

- **Get coverage whenever possible.** If your employer offers medical as a benefit, take it. Get the family on it if possible. If you loose your job, you have the right to keep your insurance under COBRA. If you don't have access to either, the your state may offer a basic medical plan with rates based upon your household income and the size of your family. Even if your employer offers you benefits, it may be more cost effective to insure your family on the state plan.

- ***Shop around.*** Most people don't realize that you can still shop around for the best price on medical care. Unless you are part of a medical co-op like Group Health, most medical plans have a list of preferred providers you may choose from. Call around before selecting your primary care physician. Some doctors will accept the portion the insurance company pays as their total bill. You may still have to make a co-payment, but they waive anything beyond the amount the insurance pays.

- ***Review your bills.*** Keep track of what the insurance company will pay and what is charged. Make sure it is accurate. Challenge anything that doesn't look right.

- ***Don't fall between the cracks.*** If you have a dispute with your insurance company or medical provider, don't allow them to blame each other and leave the situation up to you to rectify. Try to dump an uncooperative representative. Call back at different times to speak with a different person. When you get stonewalled, ask to speak to a manager. Keep kicking the issue higher until you find someone with the authority to resolve the issue. Be polite, persistent, and persuasive.

- ***Use generic medications whenever possible.*** Most major drugs have a generic counterpart. These are usually priced much lower than the brand name versions. This goes for non-prescription drugs too. Acetaminophen is just as effective when it's packed in a generic box as it is when it's labeled "Tylenol."

- ***Ask your insurance company for lower premiums.*** Make sure your level of coverage is right for your family. Most insurance companies have different levels of coverage to accommodate your specific needs. You can often save fifty or sixty dollars per month on your premium by increasing the amount of your deductible, or your co-payments. Of course, if you or your family tend to spend a lot of time at the doctor's office, you may be better off by paying the higher premiums.

- ***Stay healthy.*** The obvious way to cut your medical bills is to not owe any. Eat right. Exercise. Drink plenty of water. Cut down on the carbohydrates.

Get your vitamins. You know what you should do. A healthy body wards off sickness better than a run down tired one. Studies have shown that limiting your sugar intake helps keep your immune systems working in top shape. If you are involved in activities and behaviors that result in a higher risk of accident or disease, changing those behaviors will result in significant medical savings. Stop smoking, cut down on your alcohol intake, quit jumping out of operational airplanes, change your eating habits, that sort of thing.

- ***Uninsured? Ask for assistance.*** If you don't have insurance and you find yourself or one of your family in the emergency room, don't panic about the bills. The state may have a program that pays the bills for people in this situation. Most hospitals have a person on staff whose job it is to help you fill out the forms, and get the application process started. This could literally save you thousands of dollars, and keep you out of bankruptcy.

BEAUTY AIDS

Try coloring your own hair, or get a friend to help. However it turns out, you'll either be saving a bundle on a great new color, or making a bold new fashion statement.

- ***Try the Moonlight Special.*** Some beauticians do hair or nails on the side at home for less.
- ***Use the local beauty school.*** Many communities have a beauty school or barber's college. The students must practice on someone, and they will charge you a reduced fee to practice on you. You may feel that you should charge them for the experience, but don't worry. Their services are administered in a controlled environment, and every haircut must be inspected by the instructor. So, even if your haircut only gets a 'C', the instructor will finish the job by demonstrating what the student should have done.
- ***Do it yourself tongue piercing kits.*** Just say no.

GROCERY SHOPPING

Grocery shopping usually takes a huge bite out of the family budget. Careless shopping here can really cost you a bundle. Some strategic planning can help simplify your shopping, as well as stretch your budget to cover everything you need, and filter out expensive impulse items.

- ***Create menus ahead of time.*** Planning a prepared list of menus for a week or more gives you the power to control your grocery spending. It gives you the ability to better plan your shopping, take advantage of coupons, sales, and bulk purchases.
- ***Plan your shopping.*** Avoid running out to the store every other night. Regular shopping trips, either weekly, bi-weekly or monthly, help you control impulse buying.
- ***Use reusable products.*** Use wash rags and hand towels instead of paper products when ever possible. A paper roll of paper towels lasts less than a week in most households, while wash rags and hand towels last for years. At just a dollar per roll, you'll spend $50 per year, while a set of wash cloths and hand towels can be purchased for less than $10, and washed all year for less than $5.
- ***Use coupons.*** They do save you money. A lot of money! Recently, I bought over $90 worth of groceries for less than $30! Set up a coupon folder, and take it every time you go shopping. I use it as

part of my overall plan. Since all my meals have been planned for the week, I can take real advantage of the manufacturers coupons and in-store specials.

- ***Watch the local papers for store coupons.*** These usually come out on Wednesdays. Most supermarkets advertise 'loss leaders' to get you to come into the store. With a carefully planned shopping route, planned around your menus, you can take advantage of these.
- ***Use supermarket savings cards.*** Safeway, QFC, Albertsons and others offer discount savings to card holders. Yes, they will be able tell which brand of toilet paper you bought, but who cares? Don't forget to combine your card savings with manufacturers coupons! BONUS: Albertsons still takes coupons from competing stores (up to ten each visit), combine these with your manufacturers coupons for double savings!
- ***Use buy-one-get-one-free sales to stock up.*** Be on the lookout for special sales on those items you use a lot of. Buy in bulk when ever you can.
- ***Double up on coupons.*** Save the manufacturers coupons and use them when your store is running an in house special. Then use both coupons together. I've even been able to triple up, when I found an in store special, that I had another store's coupon for, and the manufacturer's coupon. That's savings!
- ***Try out the generic brands.*** Generic brands and store labels are a great way to reduce your grocery bill. You may find that you like some better than the name brands. Try out the cereals in the big bags on the bottom shelf in the store. They taste the same as the brand name cereals, but cost much less.

- ***Watch your store prices.*** Every store's pricing scheme is different, one dropping the price on milk this week, while the other drops the price of eggs. Plan your shopping trip to take the widest advantage of these teaser prices.
- ***Include wholesalers when possible.*** Cash-n-Carry normally caters to restaurants and other businesses, however, I've never had them turn down my money when I shop there. You'll have to buy in bulk on some items, but the prices are worth it. Another good place is the Canned Foods Warehouse, which buys closeout and damaged goods. Your cans may be bent, and the boxes may be a little scruffy, but you'll be surprised at what you find, and the savings will be well worth it. Just beware of impulse buying here.
- ***Watch out for prices that are 'after rebate.'*** That's the price only if you take the time to fill out the rebate form and send it in. They offer rebates because it makes the offer more attractive, and they know that a huge percentage of buyers will forget to send the rebate form in on time. Make sure the rebate is more than the cost of your envelope and stamp.
- ***Grand Openings usually mean super sales!*** Time to stock up! The great thing about grand opening sales is that even if the store opening is fifty miles from you, the sister stores in the area will often celebrate the opening with sales of their own.

It's easy to identify people who can't count to ten. They're in front of you in the supermarket express lane.

M. Grundler

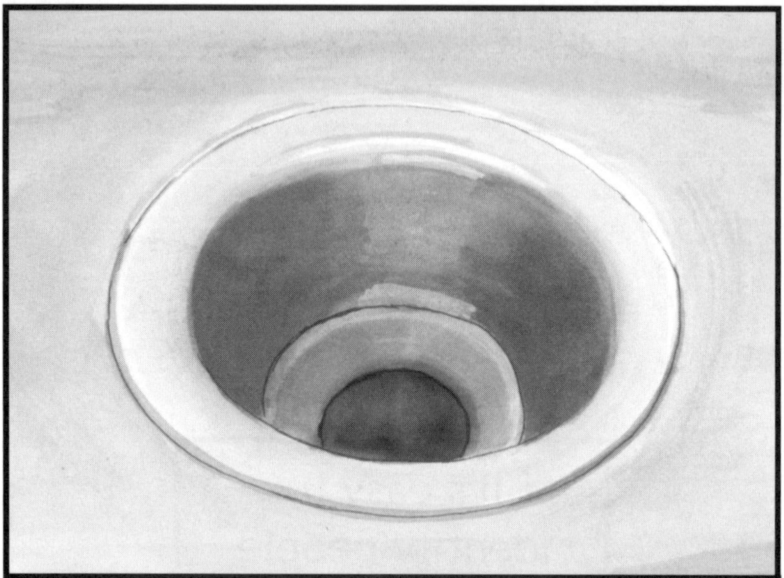

This is where your rent money really goes!

Question:

What can you get for twelve rent receipts and $3.48?

Answer:

A Grande Irish Cream Latte from Starbucks!

PURCHASING A HOME

Purchasing a home will be the single biggest purchase of your life (Unless you're in the habit of buying airplanes and large boats). If not done properly you could wind up paying thousands more than you have to. You're going to need professional advice, both from a real estate agent, and from your loan officer. You need to know ahead of time what is more important to you, having as small a down payment as possible, or having the lowest monthly payment possible. Do you want to pay points to get a lower rate? Are you willing to take a slightly higher rate in order to reduce out of pocket costs? Should you take go FHA, VA, conventional, non-conforming? These are all questions best answered with a professional mortgage broker. However, here are some rules-of-thumb to think about.

- ***Make a big down payment.*** To reduce your monthly payments, put as much down on the house as possible. If you can put 20% down, you should. The reason for this is that you can avoid paying private mortgage insurance (PMI) payments. PMI is not tax deductible. The other reason is that your mortgage payments will be much lower. You won't be making a PMI payment for one thing, and your mortgage will be based on 80% of the sales price instead of 97%. Depending upon the size of the loan this could be several hundred dollars saved each month!

- ***Make as big a down payment as possible.*** Even if you can't put 20% down, put as much down as possible. The more you put down, the less your mortgage insurance premiums will be. Again, PMI is not tax deductible. Only the interest is tax deductible.

- ***Don't skip the first month's payment.*** One of the things you may be surprised to find out when buying your home is that the bank doesn't want you to make the first payment. You take possession on July first, but you don't have to make your first payment until August first. Isn't that nice of the bank? If you think they do it so you can spend more on furniture, think again. The law says they can't charge you interest on the money you've borrowed until the end of the month, and any money you send them prior to the end of the month, has to be paid onto the principle. That would mean that if you made the payment, the entire principle and interest portion of the payment would have to go towards the principle. By doing that, you will shorten your mortgage by eight months, and save yourself over $10,000 on a $200,000 loan at 7% interest. That one early payment is equal to your first eight monthly principle payments.

- ***Double your principle payments.*** If you do not have a lot to put down, make your complete mortgage payment plus the next month’s principle for the first two years, or for as long as you can. These extra payments now will save you THOUSANDS of dollars by drastically reducing the length of your mortgage. Even an extra $50 to $100 per month over the life of the loan can shorten you mortgage by three to six years, and save tens of thousands of dollars in interest.

- ***Keep an eye on your Loan-to-Value ratio.*** When it reaches 80% or lower, you are no longer required to pay PMI. Have it removed. The lender will not watch this for you. This applies to conventional loans only, not FHA.
- ***Streamline to save.*** FHA and VA loans may be refinanced for less money than other loans. This is called "streamlining." The rules governing streamlining require the lender to charge a set fee for the process, and to use less stringent qualifications for loan approval. All that must be proved is that the home owner will save money on the new payments.
- ***Second thoughts.*** Home equity seconds may or may not be a wise move for you depending on your personal situation. If you have a lot of credit card debt or a large car payment, and you want to reduce your overall monthly payments, a second mortgage should help you reduce your monthly payments, and make your interest payments tax deductible. However, refinancing your entire mortgage and rolling in the credit cards and car payment may be an even better route, since you will get a much better interest rate. This is definitely an area you want to discuss with your mortgage professional.
- ***What's deductible?*** Remember that it is the interest rates that are tax deductible, not the entire house payment. Additionally, only interest charged on loan amounts up to the value of the home are tax deductible. Which means, if you have a second mortgage based on 125% of your home's value, only the interest charged on the portion of the loan that is below or equal to your home's value may be deducted.

- ***Watch out for Credit Card Creep!*** Thousands of people transfer their debt from their credit cards, auto loans and personal loans to a home equity loan in order to reduce their debt load and increase their cash flow. So far so good. However, many never take the next step to keep them out of further trouble: Cutting up the credit cards and closing the accounts. In some cases a lender will require this to be done as a condition of the home equity loan. However, if you have been allowed to keep the cards, keep them under strict control or get rid of them all together. If you run up amounts on the cards again, you could find yourself in an even worse position than before paying them off.

Everybody pays
a mortgage.
Renters just
pay someone
else's.
Dale Larson

Brad and Marcia eagerly awaited their credit scores.

THE SEVEN SECRETS TO SAVING MONEY ON YOUR NEXT REFINANCE

Ignorance is bliss, so we have been told. Not so when it comes to getting the best possible refinance. You can't just blindly blunder your way into refinancing your home with the first person who calls you on the phone. Who are they? Do you know them? How do you know they are telling you the truth? At the time of this writing home mortgage rates are lower than they have been at any time in the last 45 years. Every home owner in America receives an average of five calls from mortgage brokers a week. In the last decade it has become routine for a person to refinance every couple of years. If you don't know these simple strategies, you could wind up paying thousands more than you should, either in up-front fees, or in higher interest rates and higher monthly payments.

- ***Use a Mortgage Broker.*** You need someone you can trust. Someone local that you can meet with face to face, someone you can get to know on a first name basis. You need someone who knows the ins and outs of the industry leading your way. Someone who's not locked into working with any one lender. You need a professional mortgage broker. Brokers work for you, not one particular lender. A loan officer in a bank gets paid whether or not he gets you a loan. A mortgage broker only makes money when she succeeds in finding you a loan. Brokers generally have hundreds of loan programs available to them, while bank loan officers have only a handful. Banks often force you to open an account with them to get the best rate on your loan.

- ***Use an experienced mortgage broker.*** Every time falling interest rates creates a refinance market the mortgage industry turns into a feeding frenzy of shark like inexperienced sales people jumping into the market to feed on easy pickings. Last week they were car salesmen, this week they are "loan officers." The very obvious problem is that they know nothing of the business, and can jeopardize your chances of approval unless your loan fits into the "easy-squeezy" category. An experienced loan officer can find exactly the right loan for you, instead of trying to force you to fit into the only loan program he knows how to do. Unless you are trying to help cousin Ernie to break into the mortgage business, rely on someone with experience.
- ***Keep on eye on the fees.*** A loan officer should be charging no more than one "point" for the loan origination fee. A point is one percentage point of the loan amount. If he is charging more than a point "on the front" ask if he is receiving a rebate from the lender "on the back." Most lenders will pay the broker a fee to sell you a slightly higher interest rate. This can allow a broker to keep his own rates down to one point. If his rates are higher, make sure he's getting you the very lowest rate offered by the bank, and not taking a rebate from the lender.
- ***Beware of 'no fee' loans.*** Every lender has to charge some sort of loan fee to cover the costs involved in processing the loan. If they are not charging you a fee on the front, you are getting a higher interest rate than you would if you paid a fee. Possibly a much higher rate. No fee loans aren't necessarily bad, just be aware that you don't get

something for nothing. Ask your loan officer to compare the real costs between a no fee loan with a higher interest rate, and a low interest rate loan with a fee. Make sure you compare what you spend on fees with what you spend on monthly payments. Another tactic they may try is to wrap your fees up in the loan amount. If they tell you the loan will cost you nothing "out-of-pocket" it means they intend to have you borrow their fees and pay interest on them for the life of the loan! If this is the only way you can get a loan, then fine, but realize that you are paying a fee, and in this case, paying interest on that fee. Make sure you're getting a rock bottom rate.

- ***Better credit scores = lower rates.*** Credit scores have become critical measures of the probability that you will repay a loan. The higher the scores, the higher the probability you will repay. When lenders feel less risk, they lower the interest rates. If they feel threatened, they raise their rates. Credit scores have become the standardized way of evaluating the risk a particular borrower presents. Lenders now use credit scores to quickly approve high score borrowers, quickly weed out low score borrowers, and help concentrate their approval time on the moderate scoring borrowers. This has led to greater efficiencies for the lender, but sometimes the borrower feels like they have no control over the scores they receive. Fortunately you can determine what your scores will be by your financial behavior. Keep your scores up by paying your bills on time, keeping your existing mortgage paid on time, and never letting a creditor report you late. Whether you are paying on a car, a boat or your house, never let your payments get behind. Any creditor who will report your payment history must be kept happy. This will keep your scores high, and make the lowest interest rates available to you. Keep the number of credit lines to at least two but not more than four. This shows the lender you can be trusted to pay your debts, but that you don't have too much debt. Remember that credit scores take into account the last twenty four months of your financial history, so, even if you have lower scores now, you can improve them over time.

- ***Keep your LTV Low.*** The LTV or Loan to Value Ratio is the ratio between the value of your home, and amount of your loan. If you can keep your LTV below 80% you can avoid mortgage insurance and save hundreds per month on your payments. This may not be possible if you are also seeking to receive a large cash back amount. Consider taking less out, to keep your LTV low.
- ***Keep your debt payments low.*** Your debt to income ratio is one of the most important factors a lender will look at. It could determine what interest rate they will give you, or whether or not your loan will be approved. Depending on which type of loan you are seeking, the ratios will vary. However, most lenders want to see your house payments less than 30% of your total income, with your total debt payments less than 41% percent. If you're thinking of buying a car or a boat, put it off until after the loan has gone through.

AUTO-MATIC SAVINGS

Maintain your vehicle to avoid costly repairs, and keep the resale value high. This section could really be an entire book. In fact, there are books devoted to specific cars on the market, and how to maintain them. You should own the one covering your present car. These usually cost between fifteen and twenty dollars, however the information contained will make up for the expense.

- ***Change your own oil and transmission fluid.*** Learn to do the monthly maintenance on your car or truck. You'll save the cost of labor, and you can take advantage of sales on the fluids you need. If you don't know how to do your own maintenance, get a book or video from the library, or ask a knowledgeable friend to help. Purchase Chilton's manual for your car's make and model.

- ***Use a coupon and have your oil changed.*** Don't forget the value of coupons for your car care. Lube and oil places usually have some kind of promotion going on.

- ***Monitor the work.*** If you have your oil changed for you, make sure the work is done properly, and all of the advertised fluids and filters are changed or replaced. Most shops have waiting rooms equipped with a window where you can watch the work being performed.

- ***Shop around for the best service and price.*** If you need work done on your car, shop around, and get a couple of free estimates. Make sure they will do no additional work unless you approve it. If additional work is performed without your approval, complain to the manager or owner. Do not pay for the job just because it was done. If you don't pre-authorize the work, you don't owe the money.

- ***Find a repair shop that is listed with the B.B.B.*** The Better Business Bureau is a valuable resource when checking out local companies. You can access their website at www.bbb.com. If the company is listed, they will have an online history of the number of complaints received and the resolution of those complaints.
- ***Ask around.*** When looking for a car repair shop, ask your friends and co-workers for their recommendations, or warnings for that matter. Once you find a shop you can trust, stick with it.

PURCHASING A NEW CAR

Buying a new car sure is fun! Driving from one place to another, oily sales people wrapping themselves around your limbs, pushy sales managers, that new car smell, and most fun of all, haggling over the price; it all ads up to a great day on the town. Of course, if you believe that, you may also be the type that gets a kick out of home tongue piercing kits. Buying a new car is war. It's you against them, and the cards are stacked against you. So, how do you even the odds a little? Take note of these tips.

- ***Don't buy a new car!*** Ok, this does sound weird as the first tip in a section called "Buying a new car." My point here is, when you buy a new car, you will loose 20-30% of it's value as soon as you drive off the lot. See if they have demo models available that they have to sell as used. Or buy this year's model in November when they are trying to make space for next year's cars.
- ***Get pre-approved for your financing.*** This will tell you exactly what your budget is, and takes away one of the salesman's greatest tools: focusing on the monthly payment, not the price. With a pre-approval, you'll know what your maximum monthly payment will be, and you won't be fooled into haggling over payment amounts, when you should be focusing on the price of the car.
- ***Prioritize your needs and desires.*** Before purchasing a new or used car, sit down and list exactly what you want, and prioritize it into 'must

have,' 'would like to have,' and 'would be nice' categories. Use this list to evaluate each of the models you test drive. It will help you decide how much the car is worth to you.

- ***Educate yourself.*** Research the models that fulfill most or all of your requirements. Use the internet, visit car lots, read the car magazines. In this research phase, never go to a car lot with your check book in your pocket. This will keep you from buying anything on the spur of the moment.
- ***Don't be too picky.*** You shouldn't pass up an otherwise good deal because the car is lacking a couple of the bells and whistles you wanted. Use this to your advantage to drive the price of the car down, or negotiate to have the dealer add these items to the car for little or no extra cost. At worst, install these things later.
- ***Don't fall in love with the car.*** Always be ready to walk off the lot if the negotiations don't go your way. Remember, you don't have to buy a car today!
- ***Learn to negotiate.*** Your library carries books on negotiating. Arm your self with a little education on the subject.
- ***Never discuss monthly payments.*** Do your homework. Know how much the car is worth, and work on getting the price down to that amount. Don't get sidetracked by haggling over monthly payments. This is a classic trick used to keep the price high. Sure they can get the payments down, all they have to do is strap you with an extra year on the term of the loan. That extra year and extra interest payments will cost you thousands of dollars.
- ***If you can pay cash, pay it.*** If not, make as large a down payment as possible to lower your payments.

PURCHASING A USED CAR

Buying a used car is always a gamble. The trick is to minimize your risk and get the best car you can afford without getting stuck squeezing someone else's lemon. Buying the cheapest car you can find may lead to expensive maintenance costs later on.

- ***Get the best for the price.*** Look for the newest car with the lowest mileage possible. Be careful you are not buying someone else's trouble. Ok, this is the tenth time I've said something like "shop for the best price." But I'll say it again. Don't just take the first price you see.

- ***Check the records.*** Ask to see the maintenance records for the car. Can the owner show you a history of good car maintenance? Are there receipts to back up their claims?

- ***Clean = Maintained.*** If the car is clean, doesn't smell bad, and looks well cared for, chances are it's also been well maintained.

- ***Ratty, stained carpets = poorly maintained.*** If the carpets, and other upholstery are bad, it's a warning the rest of the car may not have been well maintained. Keep looking.

- ***Turn down cars that smell musty.*** Damp, musty cars are an indication that it has been sitting somewhere unused for quite some time. Beware of molds and mildews that can trigger health risks, such as asthma.

- ***Look up the car on CarFax.com***. For less than twenty dollars[15] you can get unlimited history reports on any car sold in the United States. This will tell you if the car you are looking at has been wrecked or totaled in the past. It will also list the annual licensing, and reported mileage.
- ***Pay cash or 90 days same as cash*** when ever possible to save thousands of dollars in financing fees. This isn't as tough as it sounds, if you begin planning to buy your next car a year or so in advance. Start saving for your next car well before you need it.
- ***Check out the library*** for books on buying and selling used cars. Always arm yourself with knowledge when making a purchase this big.
- ***Know your blue book pricing.*** Kelly's Blue Book, long the automotive authority on new and used car values, is now online at www.kbb.com. You can check out the value of any make and model of car. Use this information in determining if you have found a great deal, or if you are being suckered.

Drive-in banks
were established
so most of the
cars today could
see their real
owners.

E. Joseph Crossman

SO, CAN I CALL AN ELECTRICIAN NOW, OR ARE YOU AN ESCAPE ARTIST, TOO?

TAKING CARE OF YOUR HOME

Maintain your home and yard just as you would your car. If you let these go, the repairs will increase in price as time goes by. Home maintenance is vital to keeping the value of your home high, and saving money on costly repairs. Experience has also shown that well maintained neighborhoods suffer less crime than those that are not maintained.

- ***Only buy a fixer if you can fix her!*** Buying a home is no time to over estimate your handyman skills. Certainly you can save thousands of dollars on a fixer, but how much will you have to put into it to make it livable? Here's a list of things to consider:
    - Does it need cosmetic surgery, or does the house have bone cancer? Sometimes you can find a real charmer that only needs a coat of paint and some landscaping to come up to it's potential. However, that peeling paint job could also be hiding rotting beams, insect damage or a bad foundation. How can you tell? Have your home inspected before buying it.
    - Do you have the skills to handle the refurbishing, or will you need professionals? Once you know the extent of the repairs needed, take an honest look at your skills and decide how much you can take care of, and what you will have to contract out. Make sure to use this as leverage to get the best price and terms out of the seller.

  - Is the neighborhood worth living in once you've got the place fixed up? Look for the worst home in the best neighborhood you can afford.

- ***Compare pricing at the home stores.*** I keep saying this don't I. Well, it bears repeating. Always be on the look out for the best prices and discounts! Watch for seasonal sales. Take advantage of Memorial day and Labor day sales. Watch for weekly sales throughout the summer. And if anyone claims they won't be undersold, shop around and see them last. Then make them put up or shut up.

- ***Get to know how to use a hammer.*** Many home repairs are well within the range of the do-it-yourselfer. Put together a basic home tool kit, and keep it in easy reach. Most home improvement stores carry a "homeowners" tool kit that should cover your needs. These typically cost between fifteen and thirty dollars.

- ***Get a home repair manual.*** All of the large home maintenance stores carry their own version. Or go to the library and check out the books you need. Reader's Digest also publishes a very good version. These books cover the entire range of home maintenance and repair, and are well worth the cost. A friend of mine refinished all of the wood flooring in his home based upon the advice in the Reader's Digest version.

- ***Work safely.*** Make sure your tool kit includes proper safety protection. There's no sense in saving money on doing your own home repairs, if you have to spend it on emergency room visits. Always wear safety glasses or goggles when using power tools that throw off waste materials, such as saw dust, grit or sparks. Wear dust or chemical masks when working where airborne toxins are present. Make sure respirators are properly fitted, and rated for the chemicals you are using. Most important, don't skip safety to save a few minutes. Too many people wind up in the emergency ward because they didn't stop to take the time to be safe.

- ***Make sure your house is well insulated.*** Include your walls, attic, floors, pipes, water heater, windows, and doors. Check for worn or missing weather stripping, and replace it. Put up storm windows in the winter. Cover your outdoor water faucets. Interest free loans for home insulation are available from your power company. These often include money for insulation, new windows and doors, furnaces, hot water tanks, etc. Get rid of old aluminum windows and replace them with modern double pane windows.

- ***Don't ignore warning signs.*** Leaking faucets, wet cabinets under the sink, prior water damage on ceilings and any other sign of moisture are all things that should be investigated to find and fix the source of the water leak. Long term exposure to water will rot your cabinets, cause flooring to peal, damage sub-flooring and encourage the growth of molds and mildew. Replacing a bad sink seal may cost you your Saturday and a few bucks, but left undone, it could cost you thousands of dollars in repairs to your cabinetry, walls and floors.

- ***Pick up bargains at the end of the season.*** I like to decorate. I like to change my home décor by the season, and I like to have everything look neat and proper. But as you have guessed by now, I don't like the expense of decorating. So, I have developed a way to decorate my home, without spending enormous amounts on it. For instance, I may buy next year's Christmas decorations for more than 50% off after this Christmas! I do this with all holiday decorations. Well, may be not Easter eggs. You'd be amazed at what terrific items are often left over just before, or just after Christmas. And since the store is trying to get rid of these items to make room for the next holiday, you can stock up and store them for next year!

MAJOR APPLIANCE MAINTENANCE

We spend hundreds of dollars, some times thousands of dollars on our major appliances. Usually these modern day beasts of burden plod on day by day carrying their loads uncomplainingly and without trouble. But did you ever stop to think how much you depend upon them? It only takes a short blackout to make you realize how much of your life depends upon the uninterrupted service of these machines. So it is wise to keep your mechanical servants well maintained.

- ***Perform regular maintenance on your large appliances.*** Read the owner's manuals and make sure you are keeping this expensive equipment in good repair. Preventative maintenance is usually less expensive than repairing or replacing a major appliance.

- ***Get expert advice from the library.*** If you do have a major appliance go out, you can often repair it yourself with the help of a book from the library. I had a friend who extended the life of a ten year old drier with the help a library book, a couple of hours and parts costing less than forty dollars.

- ***Moving parts hate dust.*** Vacuum the back of your appliances to keep all vents and motors free from dust and heat build-up. This can help avoid costly repairs later.

- ***Moving parts hate heat.*** Make sure you have sufficient air flow around your appliances. This helps dissipate heat and prevents motors from burning out. Don't allow paper bags, fallen clothing or other debris to collect around your washer and drier. Besides being a fire hazard, they cut off the air flow that cools your appliances.

- ***Avoid costly service agreements.*** I'm constantly amused when I purchase a major appliance (or even a minor appliance) and the sales person tries to sell me an extended warrantee, often for ten percent or more of the purchase price. I always think, why am I buying this piece of junk if it will break after a year? That's what the guy is telling you, my product is so bad we have to sell extended warrantees to fix them when they die. Of course he's just spent twenty minutes explaining that this machine is the finest thing built by the hands of man. So why do you need to buy an extended warrantee? Extended warranties do one thing: they jack up the price of the product by ten to fifteen percent. Sure, the company will fix or replace your washer if the thing breaks within the warrantee period. But, how can they afford to give you a brand new washing machine that costs $399 for the price of a $40 warrantee? They know that they almost never have to pay up. That's how. They have confidence, in the appliance you just bought, and so should you.

- ***Start an appliance repair fund.*** Take the money you saved from not buying all those extended warrantees and put it into an appliance repair fund. That way, if you ever do need to fix a washer, you've already got the money to do it.

ONE LAST THING...

Well, as the porcine star of Warner Brother's fame used to say, "Th-th-that's all folks." I hope you've enjoyed reading this little volume, but more importantly, I hope you use what you've read to make your life better. But you know, the only way that will happen is if you decide to change the way you are handling your money now.

Some one once said that the definition of madness is doing the same thing over and over again, expecting to get different results. If you never change what you are doing, you will never change your situation.

Whether you realize it or not, you have a decision to make. You can put this little book down and walk away from it, forgetting everything you've read, or you can decide to act on some of the ideas presented here, embarking on a road that leads to better financial health, a better relationship with your spouse, a larger home, an island in the Caribbean, or even a ticket to the space station. Ok, maybe I've gone a little overboard here. My point is, nothing changes until you make the choice to do things differently.

I'd love to hear how these tips have worked for you, please visit my site at ***www.howtokeepmoreofwhatyoumake.com*** and drop me a line. If you've got a tip to share, you can do that too, and it may even make it into the next edition!

I'm also getting ready to write my next book called ***How To Keep Your Credit Squeaky Clean!*** Although I've got a pretty clear idea of what I think should be in the book, I'd love to know what questions you have about credit in general, your credit rating, cleaning up credit problems or avoiding them altogether. So, please give me a visit, at ***www.HowToKeepMoreOfWhatYouMake.com*** and leave me a note.

Thanks for listening, see you soon!

References

All Bible references are from the New International Version

---

[1] 1st Timothy 6:10a—Author's emphasis
[2] Proverbs 6:6
[3] Luke 6:38
[4] Luke 6:34 & 35
[5] Luke 6:38b
[6] Genesis 14:20b *"Then Abram gave him a tenth of everything."*
[7] Leviticus 27:30 & 32 *"A tithe of everything from the land, whether grain from the soil or fruit from the trees, belongs to the LORD; it is holy to the LORD. **32**The entire tithe of the herd and flock—every tenth animal that passes under the shepherd's rod—will be holy to the LORD.*
[8] Malachi 3:8-10 *"Will a man rob God? Yet you rob me. But you ask 'How do we rob you?' In tithes and offerings. **9**You are under a curse—the whole nation of you—because you are robbing me. **10**Bring the whole tithe into the storehouse, that there may be food in my house. Test me in this," says the LORD Almighty "and see if I will not throw open the floodgates of heaven and pour out so much blessing that you will not have room enough for it."*
[9] Barna Research Group, www.barna.org May 19, 2003 report entitled *Tithing down 62% in the Past Year*
[10] Proverbs 3:9-10
[11]Luke 21:1-4 *"As he looked up, Jesus saw the rich putting their gifts into the temple treasury. **2**He also saw a poor*

widow put in two very small copper coins. [3] 'I tell you the truth' he said, 'This poor widow has put in more than all the others. [4] All these people gave their gifts out of their wealth; but she out of her poverty put in all she had to live on."

[12] II Corinthians 9:7

[13] II Corinthians 9:6-11

[14] II Corinthians 9:11

[15] At the time of this writing.

Coming Soon From Doris Fitzgerald:

How To Keep Your Credit Squeaky Clean!

—Easy steps everyone can take to clean up bad, and maintain good credit.

Even if you've never experienced the embarrassment of being turned down for credit, and especially if you have, you need to read this book!

Doris Fitzgerald reveals:

- Why you should pull your own credit report, at least once a year!
- How to read your credit report
- What surprises you may find on your report.
- How to protect yourself from identity theft.
- Your rights under the Fair Credit Reporting Act
- How to dispute and remove errors
- How to interpret your credit scores
- How to improve your credit scores
- And much more.

Reserve your copy now at www.wordsofwisdompress.com.